EYES SEE SOUL

*A Journey of Personal
and Eternal Transformation*

Collected Poems of
Jhanjhri Shah

Raw Earth Ink

2021

First paperback edition July 2021

All photographs by Jhanjhri Shah
Art: "Healings from Twin Flame's Love" by unknown artist
Front cover by bookcoverzone

ISBN 978-1-7360417-7-2 (paperback)

Published by Raw Earth Ink
PO Box 39332
Ninilchik, AK 99639
www.taracaribou.com

This book is affectionately dedicated to all who got me here, my twin flame Jessica Wall who made me word my poetry, Khanjari Joshi who read it all, and Hardik Shah and Aashi Shah who are my work's forever supporters.

Table of Contents

<u>*Preface*</u>

This book is much more than a collection of my poetry.

This is an adventure of my soul's spiritual journey, marinated in incantation. It is an expedition cloaked in language that awaits your indulgence.

The excursion begins at the lowest level of being draped in melancholic clothing. It leads to an uphill battle dressed in empiricism to the highest level that affords healing to the corium with the feel of ancestral and nature spirits.

Conceivably, like me, you will experience magic of shamanic healing and be forever changed.

Life's Base Camp

Labyrinth Walk

I sense a chasm waiting for me to curvet

Not knowing the direction or path to follow

I walk like incessant steps of labyrinth many times

My poetic ossein are the seeds in dark earth

Awaiting water and sunlight to set it free

I find a door from the memory of my soul

Passage after passage, spaces start to unfold

I embark on a shamanic expedition of sorts

My perspicacity is widened through experiences

All of which I hope to carry on to the waiting page.

Recipe from Poet's Heart

A cup of imagination mixed with optimism

A tablespoon of magic dipped in perseverance

A pinch of honesty combined with the pen's ink

A touch of motivation glazed in drowning depth is

Baked in the oven of the best and worst experience

A quick prick checked words lost in flint black darkness

Became a perfect recipe fictionalized from a poet's heart.

A Cairn of Words

A poet hears the calling behind every word

I hear that call and answer with my scription

I wander the colossal landscape of my heart

To find the perfect pattern to letters' interplay

I feel the fluttering on my heart as I peel the layers

Blossoming inner flower grants me the end I seek

A cairn of words is how I form my poetry.

Ink-stained Pages

My love so deep

I put it on my body

Tattooed it with ink

Dripping from my heart

I wish to shriek

But for now

I will write it down

In the hopes that some

Will be willing to read

My ink-stained pages.

<u>*Purpose of Poetry*</u>

Strangers asked for my purpose of poetry

I explained my quandary in few words per below:

I used wise and descriptive words of other people

(People who wrote before me and write now)

To assimilate and appreciate who we are in unison

Strophe, stanza nor a song stood up to our accord

So, I write poetry to seize our forever in ways more than one.

<u>Frail Society</u>

Eyes full of gold and body full of dark

Mind made of glass and heart made of stone

Claiming to be pieces of extraordinary

Yet everything is ordinary overall

Advertising to be immortal

However, the entire existence so fleshy

Thy name is frail society.

<u>*Living Futility*</u>

Nature is the way to connect to the realm of ancestors

But what happens when you look up and see polystyrene clouds?

What happens when you sense the ghosts wired to circuit boards?

What happens when you touch the sun's turbine and catch fever?

What happens when you get swept away in night's ravenous dreams?

What happens when you get sucked in the sparkling needle of vaccine?

What happens when you think of confident thoughts of uncertainty?

What happens when you read signs to an emptiness of being?

What happens when you inhale death provoking hatred?

And what happens when you realize the life you enjoyed was merely futility you lived?

Home?

They say life is a journey

Why does my heart

Always look for someplace

That feels like home

If life is really a journey

I often times wonder

What (really) is home?

<u>Callous Darkness</u>

Setting sun satiates the elegance of the evening skies

Last hug of endearment felt from the warmth of the day

I kiss reflections of the day to wash away all sordidness

Slowly at the horizon, I witness the radiant graffiti fade away

It is now that the unapologetic night takes charge and

The callous darkness writes yet another obituary

To be posted in the filings of time.

'Her'

I am asked by many, who is the 'her' I often speak of in my poems

Today, I take time to articulate, explain and answer who she is to me

She coached me, lose your mind to find your soul and let your guard down

She guided me, connect your soul to mine and make it whole forever

She directed me, let this rain (tears) wash away your pains and aches

She read me, my book of life and showed me my mirror in her eyes

She educated me, time will remain after you and I are gone from here

I annunciate to this universe, she is truly and, in every way, my twin flame!

Autumn Breeze

Energized were my spirits

When birthing leaves soothingly

Emerged on the thorny branch

At the cautious and sensitive mien

Of a warm spring zephyr

Shattered, I found myself

When loyal summer leaves

Left their beautiful trees

At the incessant caress

Of a crisp autumn breeze.

Backstabbing

Stabbing me sharp in the back

With stellar lies and fake smiles

In a world full of irrationality

The wind demands logic

With none to understand

The rhythm of my heart

My mind avoids the dark

And my eyes seek her visual

Her words are my only solace

Finally, my pain now

Seems to lessen in a slow lento movement.

Fall in the Fall

Fall is here with its crisp climes

Leaves begin their descent

Sliding across the city's skyline

Gravitating towards a bed of rocks

Keeping the midair tryst between

Crispy cool and falling leaves

Fluidity of time is now realized

For this enormous amalgamation

The rock held its very breath

While leaves lost their own.

<u>*Half Awake Scenery*</u>

Half-awake yet asleep

Are countless lives

Walking this earth lost

Searching for a purpose

They spit their grievances

On to the screen statics

They gaze and care for

The empire of lament

Crafted from their within

With crumbled souls inside

They forget to plant seeds

Where their tears once fell.

Questions

Have you asked yourself these questions:

Do you affect people or infect them?

Are you one with and living with your higher self?

Do you understand that people and situations are powerless
without your reaction?

Have you lived the truest form of your life?

(for that is only on your dreams awake)

Have you let your emotions (energy in motion) free?

Do you partake in nature's forced fields of consciousness?

Do you react being prisoner of the past?

Or do you act to be pioneer of the future?

Ask yourself if ignorance is bliss or brutal

(for it will make you dead while being alive)

Self-inspect yourself and know that reading is fun-da-mental!

Dying Warmth

The sun shines for fewer hours

And leaves produce no chlorophyll

It is time for a dazzling leaf show

And watch foliage perform sun salutations

Everything colored in crimson hues

And infused in pumpkin spice scent

Cooler temperatures will soon settle in

Dropping leaves all over the ground

Slowly, breath will rasp out of its lungs

And everything will stand frozen

When winter inches in to feel the dying warmth.

<u>Battle Warrior</u>

Tonight, rest your warrior heart

The battle tested and wore you

You wear your wounds as medals

And their scars as ink of tattoo

This sisterhood of souls

Shows you strength and courage

To keep fighting: one day more

One hour more, one moment more.

After Me

A silent witness to my survival

Of all that the dreary world

And its lack of emotional dexterity

Changed in me to be the lady I am

But after I am gone

All that will be remembered of me

Is my written words and untold thoughts

Of love inscribed within my flesh

Everything will reduce to a moment's memory

Like what stardust leaves behind

A sense of echo of luminosity

That exists in the space between stars

I have blossomed inside her essence

And I am (erroneously) named as sky's brightest star.

Memories

Coming to me when I least expect

Distinct, beautiful and vivid

These memories…

A song, a movie, a conversation, a book

A moment, a flash in and across time

That triggers these memories

Embrace, cherish, and revel in memories.

Dad's Suit

I sing to you a requiem

For the days passed from

Existence to extinction

In this silent song, I challenge

My memories to outlive

Our father daughter love

For only time will tell

My tale of how I wear

Your chivalry as mine and

Your warrior's deftness

As my invincible armor.

A Point from Point in Time

A memory from the pages of the past

A tune from the vinyl records of recollections

A moment from when time was tender

A laughter from a place of sheer serenity

A word of care from the typewriter of reminiscence

All of them together, gently caress delicate grooves of synapses

And brings back the touch of warmth from hugs of my dad.

<u>*Finding Her*</u>

I find her in the most inconspicuous things:

It is her in the shadow of the light

It is her in the clouds of the sunshine

It is her in the warm breath of cold air

And it is her in the beating heart of a rock.

Raging Battle

I hear battle drums beat louder each day

Different cohorts settled on either side

Millennials act as cybernated warriors

Myths and lies cannot be gun powder

Hacking is not the only trigger to be used

For them, everything requires hashtags

Hashtags alone cannot be the fighters

All of this can keep the enemy busy

But more is needed to win the battle and

The battle only gets deadlier by the minute.

My Being Defined

Memories:

Sometimes they save me

Sometimes they destroy me.

Life:

Sometimes eulogizes me

Sometimes denounces me.

Stories:

Sometimes narrate me

Sometimes conceals my very existence.

Friendship:

Sometimes ornate me

Sometimes prosaically extinguishes me.

<u>*Forgiveness*</u>

I sit here lost and cold remembering the time I was a slave to the circumstance

I sit here realizing the stark honesty of when I failed her

I sit here heartily repenting my abominable behavior for I know how much I hurt her

I sit here gathering all my courage to ask for forgiveness

I sit here seeking forgiveness for it is not a feeling

It is rather a promise I make thereafter to never let her down again.

Screams

Cover your eyes often, not to hide them

But to silence them for awhile as they speak too much

Though sometimes I fear your very silence

As it can be your loudest screams

Is it your inner darkness or the empty spaces

That screams and aches for light

For that, I feel the desire to know your past

Not to punish you but to understand

How you need to be loved.

Noise of Chaos

Is it the noise of the chaos or the sound of our lives happening at once?

Is it the stain on my body or I marked my skin with your burning beauty?

Is it the salty water running down my cheeks or the lava of emotions erupting from the volcano?

Is it the hollow shell of me or the love captured self I see in the mirror?

My Script

I write for it allows me to expose the parts that compose me

I write so that the pen and paper are the witness to my vulnerability

I write for my words to be a haven for my raging storms and an abode to my dreams

I write so that I can experience true limitlessness of emotions

I write so that I can vocalize the story of shades, voices and giving life to death

I write so that she lives forever, and her memories never die

I write to find a gateway through which she knows who she truly is

I write because writing is my true sanctuary where we amalgamate.

Sunsets

Sunsets, end of the day for most but a beginning of an entire new era for me

An era that is my escape to the reality that dwells deep within

An era that gives me every chance to live the sojourn abyss of time

An era where my solitude guides my path to reach the stars and galaxies that shine relentlessly

An era that symbolizes a promise of a new dawn at the twilight of its life.

Questions for Uncivilized Civilization?

Today, I sit here whittling away

The residue of yesteryear

Struggling to answer these questions:

Do I need to ask for forgiveness?

For when you imbued my veins

With your corruptive hatred

Do I need to ask for forgiveness?

For when you pervaded my marrow

With your concentrated evil

Do I need to ask for forgiveness?

For when you invaded my thoughts

With everything that haunted

Today I sit here starting afresh

With a new version of truth

With a new shade of light

That allows me to let go of

Your darkness as I enter another episode

And resume all that was out on hold by you.

<u>*Frozen*</u>

Will our magic die in below freezing temperatures?

Will our happiness sway away by the passing arctic storm?

Will our laughter stand still like fingerprints on a frozen tenement window?

Will our friendship paralyze like hominid footprints destined to be discovered only in the poetic embryo that spawns anarchy?

How Can I?

How can I drag her light into the darkness I emit?

How can I tie her wilderness in the rope I hold?

How can I croon to her melodies into the noise I am?

How can I hold her successes into the impediment I am?

Gift

Do I gift you the flowers plucked from the earth that start wilting and rotting the moment they leave the comfort of the soft soil?

Do I gift you the light from the orb of the day that starts enervating and weakening the second it leaves the warmth of the shining sun?

Do I gift you the infinity from the ocean that starts facing and dwindling the moment it reaches the inescapable horizon?

Or do I gift you the sweet present from my happy status quo that start evanescing and eluding the second it becomes a return ticket to a moment otherwise gone?

Can You?

If I am the cracks where scars used to hide,

Can you be the flowers that now bloom there?

If I am pieces of flesh put together,

Can you be the melodies that echo deeper than the skin?

If I am the brail of scents,

Can you be its beautiful transcription that adds perfect grace to Spring?

If I am a girl full of poetry,

Can you be the one to read our story to the world?

Emotional Literature

The morning fog questioned the clarity of my vision compelling me to look beyond what my eyes could see

Suddenly, a wildfire of sun rays emerged from the frozen horizon demanding my submission to battle my unfelt emotions

Her mellifluous music slowly etched beautiful lostness on me making path that led me to her

In lostness, I found myself awaiting her text after an incomplete conversation the previous night

My frivolous and untamed thoughts wanted me to abscond the morose realities and be sequestered in doubts of: if I ever hurt her feelings

The dusty leaves carrying the scent of fear confirmed my very notion and made their way to the ground passing by me

Chirping birds whispered a sensation of my ill doings in my ears staging my urge to apologize at the forefront

I raced the squirrels scurrying for cover to account for and express regret for my misdeeds

It is then, my pen's ink and paper registered yet another emotional literature of my creation.

True North

No compass in this world could tell me where to go

No arrow ever pointed to the true north of right direction

No star shined enough to guide my path through the dark

Addicted to aimlessness that I tried hard to avoid

I closed my eyes with a leap of faith and jumped in the obscure

Only to find my direction magnetically leading up to her.

Emotions Sitting at My Windowsill

Tormented darkness relieves itself from the nightly duties

The sun rises but hates traveling through the city's urban decay

The fading moon taunts the mankind to slaughter their mountainous dreams

Caged in these four walls, let me suffocate in your breath

Locked pupils gaze your bowlike lips

Strangulate me with your unforgiving beauty

Hardened heart feeds my pen's thirst with the bloody ink

Making way for poetry: my only abode during this morning turmoil.

Good Evening Mr. Moon

Sprinkle some of the spirits where time has no use tonight

To seemingly wash away the unseen blemishes of the day

Happiness, an illusion in your eyes

Light, a mirage in your smile

You can chain my soul but let my mind free

For I do not want to breathe

But still want to dream of her dreams.

Ahead of the Horizon

Often times, I wonder what lies ahead of the horizon

Is it pouting uncertainty that quietly sips on all beer?

Is it unfaltering hope (a cicerone) that is a solace to all humanly dreams?

Is it scowling disquietude that harbingers death and decay?

Or is it limitless optimism (a connoisseur) that only tastes victory of earthlings?

Often times, I wish to see what lies ahead of the horizon.

<u>*Flight of Separation*</u>

Next year, my muddy shoes will still carry signs of last summer

I boarded the last flight of separation to one of the finest cities

The flight made its way from among the graffitied walls to

A land of dreamy forgetfulness to plant new beginnings

But you are still my favorite thing to hold onto just above

The beautiful eidetic memories when we felt each other's true emotions.

Sundown – My Dance Floor

Sun shines loud in summer

But society's demons shout louder

Falling humanity shatters on impact

Reflecting rays focus on bending the reality

Trying its life to convince all

Past is all that is left of me

I pinch the sun to rest so that

Society is forced back to its nest

Sundown is my dance floor

To sing, perform and live galore.

Rain Turned into Hail

Pounding heart and restless breath

I narrated my stories in depth with

Sadness that my past holds

Flash of memories I then unfolded

Every breath, a risk I inhaled

Every day, rain turned into hail

She promised me the vision of horizon

Hopes alike the rays of sun

Dreams that ignite my soul

She vowed, never to be a ghoul.

Waiting Room of Purgatory

A paramour dressed in Monday blues

I start my drab walk in whorls (of zero)

The clouds are muting the sun today and

In twilight of the mistakes made so far

I must inhale this universe of ache

It feels like I am consuming the leftover time

That leads to a waiting room of purgatory

This blighted condition has only one recourse:

I must standby to be emblazoned in day's monochrome.

Rains of Ruined Sorrow

On the horizon I see:

A slow awakening dawn

Shy and sleepy sun

Stormy silver clouds

With thunder in its belly

A steady buzz of beware

Ringing in my ears

Locked up in solitude

Only darkness on spare

A spark of curiosity

Questioning this atrocity for

The day forecasted for flames of sun

Lightning strikes

And now I know

It was my eyes that

Rained of ruined sorrow.

<u>*Silver Tinted Horizon*</u>

Sitting on the empty bench of a withered tree

I envisage silver tinted horizons take over

Impassioned crescendo of colorful flora

Bitterly cold winds rumble an aubade to her wake

Snow laden tree branches sparkle and radiate

Misty memories of all bygone times

Wild blue yonder with its incandescent fire

Finally makes its appearance to imprint the kiss of winter.

Surgical Cuts

They flagrantly pour salt

On the precise surgical cuts

Made in my heart over the years

It will be cold here from now on

For they can only chase

The heat of my memory

Their swirling words spoken to me

Will now haunt all their sentient life forms.

<u>Hug Goodbye</u>

In this world, in this truth

A drink of revelry makes me maudlin

In this world, in this truth

Cold fingers of decadence asphyxiate me

In this world, in this truth

Forked tongues exchange empty farewells

In this world, in this truth

I eagerly wait for her venerable hug goodbye.

Towards the Other Side

As I walk towards the other side

Paintings expel colors without reserve

Screams escape my nights without confute

Letters evict words without refute

In this state of tumult

How can my mind sleep soundly through the night?

Choosing Between Mind and Heart

Every time I write, I give out a little of me to the void

The void that exists on the silent and blank pages of my penancing book

Every time I write, I feel this strange yet familiar burn

Burn of annihilation that chars the core of my poetic nucleus

Every time I write, is a trial for me to seal my fate

Fate that pleads to place a kiss on her fetching lips

Every time I write, I tell myself; written words are a treasure

A treasure that collects and rises from love beyond eyes

Every time I write, warped in good intentions are my acts and words

Words that transpire and teach me:

Choosing the mind is intelligence but

Choosing the heart is wisdom.

The Aisle

How can I make it through to you?

I have much to pass, cover and cross

Empty faces staring from the aisle

Flashing lights throbbing the aisle

I see you towards the end of the aisle

Beauty to the beast that is the aisle

I present you my collection of the aisle

A bouquet of memories from the aisle.

<u>Rusted Rainbow</u>

In the avalanche of past mistakes

Amidst the fatigued empathies

I saw a rusted rainbow in golden rays

It was devoid of breath of fresh air

I lend my gasp and was rendered empty

I saw debris and turmoil along the way

I begged for efforts towards discovery

My warrior spirit wanted to overcome

The suffering, confusion and obstacles

So, I embodied my shield to fight the war

Between hatred and my life's purpose

Promptly, my demons were declared castrated.

<u>Season of Prime</u>

Covered in colors of this season of prime

My words are configured as zentangle art but

My emotions are shaped as being putrescible

My hushed tones are constructed into polyphony but

My dreams are added as vivid based on astrology

My colloquy is guised as preachings of a guru but

My doings are mocked upon the cracks of reality

My confab is sermonized as framed memories on the wall but

I am reduced to and worthed by my poetry, confounded as harangue.

<u>*White Corpse like Emptiness*</u>

Fall evaporates after sparking violently

Yesterday slips through my fingers

Leaving a mark of shelved stories

Winter makes its quiet comeback

Leaving its mark on my front door

Smoke from the chimney drifts

Leaving a mark of its burnt impulse

Scalding rain and snow stings the world to sleep

Leaving a mark of white corpse like emptiness

I now must relearn to breathe

Leaving the mark of choking silence.

<u>*Last Touch of Day's Skin*</u>

As the day breathes few of its last breaths

A state of painless purgatory conquers that sun-stained tiresome
day

As trees feel the last bits of the day's skin

Beautiful dark clouds unburden the sunlight to finally rest for
the night

And as I bid my farewells to all my doings that belong to the
day

I patiently wait with my arms wide open to welcome the sparkle
of the night to take charge and rule away.

Sky's Wet Canvas

God lowers a silver parachute over me such that every feeling I ever know is up in that sky

Twinkling joyful wisps of bright sunlight tear up my airy giggle clouds in totality

The persistent rain knows on every hidden entrance of my heart allowing the amalgamation of my very own thoughts and feelings

The quiet rain seems like a secret language that whispers sentiments of people who love culture

Pounding wet misery for most, yet a state of complete trance for me that celebrates springtime of my ultimate being.

Darkness, My Well Wisher

Darkness is my true well wisher

It powers my inner light and love

I whisper in ears of the passing winds

Silence answers back through my epiphanies

I walked out of all relations (but one with her)

Saying I have done all I could do here

This left behind a famine of my saved tears

To water the seeds of my personal growth.

<u>Bright Horizons</u>

Sitting on the pavement by the curbside, I watch:

Brick and mortar breed filth and crime

It is concentrated evil that throbs and beats

Blames laugh at lame jokes of misunderstanding

Deluding the obtuse, toxins adopt the course

Blistered egos voyage through blight on flotillas

No contrition or dejection for any ill doings

Altruism of plebeians are moribund

Bruised and exiguous manumission in sight

I pine for days with cerulean skied virtue, iris violet rectitude, and sunlit crimson licitness.

Dredging the Dusty Avenue

World of memories is a beautiful place

Capturing life's moments in compartments

Clearing the murky fog of oppression

Humming incantation in musical notes

Washing away today's stifle illusions

Dusting the out of reach smile and

Touching the intangible lapse of time.

<u>*Rise of a Lioness*</u>

Bucket of tears donated by my fragile heart for my past

Rescued by the fleeting fear buried under my fingernails

They say, I have always belonged in these beautiful bones

New skin cells replacing the battle-scarred ones are

Truly the markings of the warrior I have proudly become

Slowing the waking dawn senses the beginning of my smile

Rising above the horizon is a lioness in sight.

Towards Jubilance Boulevard

I am often told:

You keep your bright light on serving as a lighthouse to many who
Find their way home in the strongest of their life storms

You keep your golden heart on serving as a treasure to many who
Find your love and forgiveness in the box that carried malice and hurt

You keep your soothing rain on serving as dew drops to many who
Finds flowers amongst thorns in the driest desert of emotions

You keep the smile in your eyes on serving to your soul for those who
Find warmth among the coldest of wintery blizzards

I find and scribble my words
Before complacency eats them all.

Trail to Exultation

I leave fragments of my being along every trail I follow

Little pieces of my soul are etched onto every mountain I climb

In return, the essence of life is filled deep inside my marrow

I can sense the air and clouds working in synchronicity

I feel the chemical reactions and changes in my own atmosphere

Everything is changed just by a morning hike to the mountain top.

The Feel of Emerald Rays

They speak insolently of

Their failed beings

Their obsidian hearts

Malice filled on inside

Forgotten yesterdays

Desultory tomorrows

Their fate emblazoned

Beware of black holes

That swallow disconsolate

For their incandescent light

Is glacially diminishing

The godless creatures

Have no hope to survive

I descry approaching moments

Where effulgence eagerly

Pursues my soul

Coercing my heart

To feel the emerald rays

To birth love and light

For this offbeat humanity.

Ever Forgiving Chai

Chai is an emotion and a comrade integral to my being

It is soothing words of a letter written to my neurons

It nudges my fortitude to express itself without reservations

In times of winter, it burns stronger to cool my bones

Provides forgiveness to me when I flub everything

It successfully pulls me upward with its true devotion to serve

Lost in answering the mysteries of life, my chai:

Is empathetic and brings me back home again.

Turning Towards Singularity Lane

I drove away from the wet pavemented shore

And lost the signal to the chaotic world

As final goodbyes kindled the fire inside

I commenced my long-awaited journey

Towards the arrant certitude of singularity

I channeled my hysteria and ardor to purge fret

My mind sight created a limpid lens to observe

The truth to create my reality while being awoke.

At the Top of Exhilaration Trail

I walked up the trail to the mountain top

Emotions flood my soul through every step

I felt adrenaline build and rush through veins

Making its way and gushing without a sway

The trail was meant to travel and lead the path

I followed the course with no preset reservations

I heard the dulcet voice of an angel throughout

I held on to everything she had to say and offer

She called me home to where I have belonged

I am meant to continue and harmonize with my path

The thickets by the trail nourish and foster my soul

They took a part of me and offered a relic in exchange

Finally, I felt the freeing that I seeked within

I walked up the trail to the mountain top

Where I reached the birth of my soul's peak.

Standing Question

Misery loves company is the motto that prevails when

Darkness overtakes light hoping

I will give up on my hopeful steps

Assuming I am a broken girl

The lurid flames of fire fervently displays

My distorted shadow and mental anguish already set to purge

My anxiety sighs in relief realizing all that is needed

Is an introspection and a hopeful transfusion

The real question stands:

Am I a happy and satisfied girl who has everything she ever asked for?

Or am I a beautifully broken girl with abundant hopeful words?

<u>*From a Mile Away*</u>

An evening stroll on the streets of the city

I inhale secondhand cigarette fumes

Setting sun casts shadows behind my back

Cold flashes trap beneath my warm skin

Muck boulevards and graffitied walls are its heart

That continuously pump unceasing chaos in life

Insanity, a constant companion walks hand in hand

I see silent woes and dormant smiles from a mile away

I am the odd one out, is not a well-kept secret anymore

My way is in the mountains away from this populace.

<u>*Perfecting My Being*</u>

I see north winds blowing and whispering magic into southern scapes

I blank my soul and offer it as the canvas for the north winds to etch galaxies on it

Gradually, I am learning what it feels like to anoint, sanctify and be satisfied

Each day I hold onto the puff of wilderness to fill my lungs with hope and dreams

I look at the colors on the horizon to create imageries of truth hidden in my poems

She innerstands my vivid images while others besmirch them with muffled screams

I can accept a compliment from her without feeling like a thief stealing others' belongings

She has helped me learn: My heart's light is the only key card to a rabid journey to find and perfect my being.

Wilderness – The Gentle Balm

Shades of gray are thrown over my incandescent light

I quietly fold within myself to scrutinize these conflicts

There are reasons I choose to be invisible

I observe the masses glint their sameness

Surrounded by camera clicks noise on all sides

There is no sound of intellect and foresight

Doltishness takes on a constant seat in the show

This construct feels cold, foreign and alien

I gather, anything that just costs money is cheap

My soul hankers its only tonic – the wilderness

It holds my only weakness – undomesticated beauty

What has aged in nature is classified spellbinding

Skeleton trees flaunt the beauty of their bare arms

Mountains embody strength weathering the dust on the wind

Wilderness is gentle balm that subdues the cruelest monsters

It helps us peel back to the bark of our purest roots

The tangibility of my existence is now sterilized

Readying me to debunk the importance of plastic legacy.

Emerald Sky Cries

Breathing in snowflakes I look up north

The emerald sky cries for the lame and lost

Why does it weep for one with no shame?

Are the cries out of love and care or pain?

Will I ever know the right reason or name?

For now, I will enjoy nature's beautiful game

And bask in the warmth of these emerald lights.

Processing Shambled Thoughts

An impromptu hike in the open woods

I surrender myself to mother nature

I process my shambled thoughts

To become singular and in unison

With everything at my eyes' periphery

I do not hear steady rhythm of my footsteps

There is no better way to just be

For the placid breeze helps move

The boat of my dreams to reach

The long-awaited shores of reality.

<u>*My New Constants*</u>

There is a potion that I add to my charisma

That is the perseverance to fight the good fight

Fight to find hope, peace and love is now a constant

It often feels like walking against the tsunami

I have hope that I will carry love that shines

I have hope that I will find peace on the other side

I have hope that I won't fall for reapers on the way

I have hope that I will come out on the right side

I have hope that I will bid my negativity a farewell and

I have hope that I will find tranquility in my own being.

Questions Conflicting My Reality

I am constantly told to live in the real world

But this is the most fake world I have seen

Should I continue to live in my dream world?

I am consistently told to forget the past times

But the time is now, and this is where I love

Should I continue to create my future from here on?

I am conditioned to fill my pockets through jobs

But I fill my soul through my adventures

Should I continue my journey filled with explorations?

I am constantly asked to pick my soul color

But I swing on the multicolored rainbow

Should I continue to produce my unique colors?

I am constantly coerced to tape my broken pieces

But I celebrate each of them as my pieces of art

Should I continue to let light shine through my art?

<u>Surrender – The Real Power</u>

Emptiness fills gravity deep in my lungs

Doing nothing about it risks suffocation

So, I hold onto my pieces I have and

Travel far off to where I need to be

I open my close fists to rest my palms

I sit, surrender and touch the soil

(that once promised me to heal)

It hands me lost pieces of my construct

It touches my skin to keep the promise

I set down my wounds and pain to

Walk without the memory of its occurrence

I am boldly able to make my way towards

A future dancing like a flame in distance.

Decoding Secret Language

Star tapestry is capable to decode and comprehend:

Secret language of my footsteps on the trail

Expose the baggage I carry, to uncloak my identity

Reveal the iron strength of my warrior soul

Transport me to a land beyond the heavy mist

Devoid me of maturity in exchange of wisdom and

Grant a fierce will for my deeds to echo my heart.

Gold Brown Pyramid

The gold brown pyramid speaks a sacred pattern

It teaches my heart to listen and wield the magic it already knows

It awards me (much needed) courage to face the shadows and

Fight the unknown terrors seething beneath my mortal skin

It tutors me to shed my longings and moves in my words

It captures the song of poet's heart in a subtle rhythm

My mind and heart are left untamed and broad as forgotten lands

Turning the deepest of darkness into a promise of Spring.

Birthday Thoughts

Lighthouse of love conquers the night sea

My dreams and hope wake up under the deep blue sky

Dominion of my captivating demons gradually diminish

I gather all my peace into a different me

Until my past barely recognizes me

My frazzled insecurities dry, curl and fold elegantly

Ready to shamefully hurl into the ground

Camouflaged in greens, stoical societal stance make way

But my sanguine melody dejects birthday thoughts

As getting older and aging instead

It is experiencing, learning and evolving.

<u>*Loneliness or Freedom*</u>

With planetary axis at a tilt

The determined tree originated

It kept rising in wilderness and

Enjoyed its very own company

It chose its direction to expand

Decided never to settle for less

It loved happily under the sun and

Dreamt of the day under the moon

They called it loneliness but

For the tree, it was its own freedom.

Rusty Hinged Doors Opened

I opened the rusty hinged doors

To enter the woods by the lake

I ripped apart every band aid

Once thought would heal wounds

I found scars of a cluttered heart

I washed away the regret and hate

I dusted the cobwebs off my soul to

Create space for me and my existence.

"Healings from Twin Flame's Love"

<u>*Who is a Twin Flame?*</u>

I sense a strong connection beyond blood and race

I am connected by our energies and vibrations

You intuitively answer my silent calls

(though quantum communication)

You bring unconditional love and support

(at perfect times)

We share an unspoken level of innerstanding

You are my reminder from the universe

That on the deepest level of our existence

There truly exists another soul

That I can call as my twin flame.

Her Teachings

At the peak of dawn, the city vapes over its flame like Fall colored trees

Lake water reflects the faint skyline as a mirror on the surface

But it is also my door to another (completely different) world:

A world where the beatings of my heart dance to the rhythm of hers

A world where she is fluent in the language of my soul and sings the ballad like no one else

A world filled with perfect limitlessness where she teaches me the importance of growing wings than planting roots to stand tall yet completely motionless.

Her Preponderance Melodies

Scrapping away the pestilent

The cigarette smoke enamors the dusk invested road corners

I caress the blue-sky horizons while gazing into the silhouette of her eyes that adorn the evening

The ocean water at the beach unequivocally pleads me to transform to a lost being

It is then I fathom:

She slowly escorted me through the acrimonious reality

The alacrity of her being reminds me of the outlier I have been since birth where only words accept me for who I truly am

Furthermore, the doves and I talk in undertones shamelessly acknowledging the inescapable reality

She is an assiduous soul friend

Suddenly, her preponderance melodies among other noises ask, "What's up... What's going on?"

How do I disclose:

It is never quiet here as the words quarrel inside my head

Let us rest easy for now as the night awaits new poetry.

Haunting My Demons

The droplets of her smile extinguish the conflagration in my veins

The peace in her heart haunts the existence of sadness parading around my being

Her gentle voice coerces the demons full of adolescent angst to make their departure

The vaunted beauty of her eyes digress the callous fiend to search for a victim other than my existence

The purity of her thoughts washes all doubts that cling on to my feet

Her happiness elates the very essence of my beating heart and her touch leads me to solace like no other.

She is...

She is everything and a bit of everything feels the distress

She shines in the night and moonlight feels the shame

She breathes hope and all other breaths feel the hopelessness

She is the perfect rainbow, and all colors feel the chaos

She is a wonderful mystery that no man can ever completely unfold.

Nighttime Poetry Shenanigans

As the day signals retirement for the time:

She smiles once and the sky blushes all shades of love

One last time she looks at the mirror addicted to her happiness

She lays in the bed and sets the night demons to a captivating freedom

It is my time to guard and the sense of that duty beckons the poetry within.

Breath of my Soul

Tidal waves crash and sound like violins echoing in dreams

Oceans remain breathless while I hold on to your first heavenly sight

The cool breeze burns boiling inside my veins and creates this everlasting love

The shining water magically and calmly erupts emotions that feed the breath within my soul.

<u>*Prerogatives of a Twin Flame*</u>

Privileged I am to be permitted to be her twin flame

I pledge to place her smile in my heart and her happiness in my soul

Even my solitude will look for her

Because if not, I will be something frozen in the world that is on fire

However, if that flamelike chaos is my destiny, then let me bleed poetry.

Time – A Shameless Sentimentalist

She is the music to a life that had only known silence

She came in as a dulcet melody

She is the angel who carries me home every night

Beside whom I sleep languidly

In her presence the dark nights do not ache for the gleaming sunshine

For her beauty graces each of sun's rays

It is for her, that time itself pauses and chooses to be a shameless sentimentalist to tell her story to the world.

My Moon

She is the glow of my soul

The light of my heart and

The wildest of my pulses

I bask in her light and ethereal beauty

She is distant but nevertheless beautiful

The light of her divine being

Could put a hundred candles to shame

Madly drawing me to her heavenly persona

She is sheer brilliance on earth

And I call her my moon.

Her Promises

If I poured out my heart, she promised to drink it and not stagger

If I found myself in darkness, she promised to fill my soul with light

If I felt drenched in doubt, she promised to clear the clouds and allow my glory to shine

If I wandered away in distance, she promised to bring me back home safely.

<u>*My Soul Soaring*</u>

Her eyes efface all beauty

The sparkle in her eyes

Help digest the matte world's fallacy

A place where all can visit

But very few can enter

Her eyes when I enter

Emancipates me from life's mayhem

Without words, her eyes

Use pantomime to express

The deepest thoughts and feelings

And it is the lens of her eyes

That inspires my soul to keep soaring.

Her Clairvoyant Visions

My soul cherished her presence on the days where melancholy resided in my morose veins

My heart adored her existence on this planet in the nights where the moon hid behind my darkness

But my being was different in her occasional clairvoyant visions and

Her immortal touch only amplified the truth of her visions

I often wondered if she is the angel that plundered all agony or my remedy for everything positive

Her comforting looks erased my tragedy and washed me sin free

Now my poems beg for her compassion to stay stagnant as they have found their way from putrid to pristine.

Poet: A Photographer of Emotions and Thoughts

Bruised heart and lost in my quietness

My breath was my only escape

It was time to undress my soul from the anguish

Her light made its appearance and

My twilight felt the relief of ending

The spirit of her music engulfed my lonesome silence

The warmth of her eyes melted the iceberg of my solitude

My frosted presence drowned, and my amiable, unassuming self was born

Now I capture and break down my life in moments

For I am a poet – a photographer of thoughts and emotions.

<u>*Printing My Paper*</u>

My drive on the highway of life

Drove me to an unavoidable stop

I stood at the edge of the world

Something so far in distance

Yet situated so close to me

I breathed it in my lungs and

Felt it in my burning veins

It was her mind's guise that

Entertainingly kept me imprisoned

It was her sparkling eyes that

Served trust on a silver platter

It was her silence,

A clever ruse that willingly

Weighted me down to submission

All to lay out the secrets held in

My pen and the ink stained the paper.

<u>Weather Forecast Changes</u>

The sun rose above the horizon questioning its existence as she
made her way from asleep to awake

Prevailing winds urged to hold on to the feeble remains of her
scent as she sprinted across the walkway

Dark gray clouds escaped their ordinary course as she flew
above them avoiding the rain

Soon, she had changed the weather forecast from
thunderstorms and rain to sunny with clear skies.

Sip of Tranquility

She is the life that the edge of sword is terrified to touch

She is the light that every speck of darkness fails to conquer

She is the ink that each cell of parched paper feels desperate to meet

She is the bloom that slanders all freckles of storms

She is a sip of tranquility that a lamenting heart devours

She is, who I write about in the midnight hours where only those plagued by art are wakeful.

<u>Peering In, I See</u>

From the outside, peering in I see:

Her light keeps the midnight darkness at bay

Her voice swallows the remorseless silence of the dark

Her smile assimilates the frozen stars that camouflage joy

And her eyes reflect the nights' shameless existence where it aches for its own demise.

Immortality

Her love is a magic that binds

Eternity between our bodies

We summon our worlds to cast

Each other's names reaching immortality

Her love touches me and strips me

Layer by layer through my bones

Through my muscles and my tissues

Her love is a symbol of journey

And a timeline to our interminable lives

Such that each night I tuck her dreams

Into my bed and blanket them with faith

Her love embraces my soul and touches my scars

Worthy of my everything lunatic

She enables me to

Inhale the future and exhale the past.

<u>The Novice Boulevard</u>

I find myself on the tender age of hope

As night stretches longer each coming night

I listen close to the old ones who speak through me

They guide my steps on the Novice Boulevard

They shape my will for the uphill battle

They teach me victory of the war within

They afford me to feel the peace of relentless change

Today, it feels like the North carries my soul

I carve my trail and it carves my name in return.

Esoteric Bindrunes

Each step upward uses an ounce of my power

At the pinnacle's cusp I reach to have no power

I surrender all I am to the greater (than me) power

Esoteric bindrunes are then inscribed on with power

I cherish those as tattoos on my soul's power

I start my downward progress with renewed power

To process the ethereal talisman's true power

At the base, I know how to grow in dark's power

From the hidden quiet, new fate births to take power.

Sun's Soul Tickled

Waking up from my marmalade dreams

My mornings dripped in honey

The toasty day that lies ahead

Promises me of juicy successes to triumph

The rising sun senses a dearth of a boost

And then the warm horizon

Tickled the sun's soul to shine at its best.

All Shades of Golden Glitter

Sealing the night

With drops of hot wax

From the burning candle

I offer my heart to

This freshly waking dawn

I sense a great change

An exchange of promises

Between my soul and horizon

New beginnings unlock within

Sunlight now wraps itself

Around my little world

Allowing the warmth of love

To both, gleam and sparkle

In all shades of golden glitter.

A Colorful Kaleidoscope

Every emotion you have ever felt

Are colors from and of your soul

Be grateful for the spectral light painting

That your heart is creating and waiting

For the mornings when your eyes

Open and witness the beautiful

Kaleidoscope of colors unfurl

On the canvas of your heart's masterpiece.

Hidden Code of Survival

There is a flame burning on the inside

That has always refused to be tamed

Life's pitter patter raindrops fail to extinguish it

For it adds extra beauty to the crown I wear

It is the hidden code of survival in quiet storms and

Eases the sharp edges of turbulent winds

Now, every moment feels like a moment of rebirth!

Possessions in a Rucksack

No Groupons or discounts offered at the time

I paid for my mistakes to awaken and arise

People come and complain to me thinking

I will sit, listen, and agree to all that pessimism

But that is no longer (a part) in my pedigree

All my possessions are now packed in a rucksack

I can sit and watch the horizon, sunrise, and sun set

Realizing if some (thing/one) is not in my life

Either I do not need that, or it is not meant to be

I have already experienced and purged to ascend

I now live a life of faith, faith in my energy to soar

And she quietly initiates that elixir every day.

Instead, I Will...

I cannot keep the rain from falling in this forest

Instead, I will wear hope and always bring warmth to your soul

I cannot keep your worries from piling up

Instead, I will climb the mountain top and help shed your pain
in the waterfall

I cannot keep you from falling into pieces

Instead, I will instill love in all your pieces and lead you to peace

I cannot keep you from being silent amongst these rattling
sounds

Instead, I will bring poetic justice to unfold the enigma you
truly are!

The Race I Won

After enduring months of suffering when

My eyes burnt from gasoline tears

A deluge of happiness hits my heart

I breathe this fresh air in my lungs

Bury your hate and anger in your gut today

I don't accept consolation for the race I won

For I have fought like hell for this happiness.

Reached Ataraxy

I am paralyzed by the sight of the moon having a silver shiver

Bewildered by halogen glow, will this night's chill ever melt?

Do I now fall apart, be a part or choose to not be a part of this turpitude?

These gelid invites me to home in with a cloud of silence in its existence

It calms my ever-racing heart and tranquilizes my overthinking mind

Finally, my race to ataraxy is over and I am silently quiet on the inside.

Life's Moments in Compartments

World of memories is a beautiful place

Capturing life's moments in compartments

Clearing the murky fog of oppression

Humming incantation in musical notes

Washing away today's stifle illusions

Dusting the out of the reach smile and

Touching the intangible lapse of time.

<u>*Rain on the Inside of Umbrella*</u>

When it rains on the inside of your umbrella:

Have an abundance of love through turmoil and sadness

Have an abundance of patience during times of utmost uncertainty

Have an abundance of light peeking through the darkness

Have an abundance of hope in every given and passing moment.

Her Generous Givings

She guided me to learn the creation of smile for all the times I sobbed my fears

She comforted me with the blanket of joy for the moments I encountered horrors

She helped me master the meaning (and spelling) of acceptance for all my blues I saw in the mirror

She lifted me to wonder the real deeds of self for all the epiphanies I am hope kissing humankind.

<u>Pardon My Poetry</u>

Pardon my poetry that writes of you and nature

Where bookmark leaf covets every scribbled page

Do not worry my love, this love

Is certainly not a once upon a time thing

I write not in pencil but in blueberry ink

Shards of our love still linger the coffee shops

That once twinkled and smelt of our ubiety.

Riding on Love Lexicon

Writers write of the stories that live on the dark side of the crescent moon

I write of your love that flows through my veins

My heart poundingly beats into the timeless happily ever afters

That start with a spark of authenticity and honesty open to life's trust tortures

Fed upon realities of legitimacy and continue to ride on love lexicon.

<u>*From the Doorstep of the Soul*</u>

You are the silhouette of the vision

That you had since you were a kid

Stand under the light to add details

On the middle/inside of the shadow self

Color yourself with your purpose

Leave all that harms on the outside

Touch and feel the reality of life

Progress from the doorstep of the soul

Enter the wormhole to link to the Source

Become and evolve into you(rself).

My Dear September

My dear September,

You are fully surrounded by the winds of change

You carried away the lingering warmth around me

You made sure to leave a cold swift to bask in

You brought a chill to touch and freeze my soul

Yet, I fought and grew from when we met last year

I developed a sun of my own to spread the warmth

I gently offer you this warmth so you can feel again.

<u>*Release Emotions Through Poetry*</u>

With life comes death but

Rebirth is real if you:

Let fluidity shape your essence

Let love nurture your growth

Let empowerment rule your desire

Passion fire your actions

Kindness raze your avarice

Futility engulf your flaws

Introspection improve your quintessence and

Poetry releases your emotions.

The God(ly) Element

Ticking of the clock is synchronous to the beating of my heart

Clock's time and heartbeat's throb busy being loyal

To their very own peace of mind

By focusing purely on their purpose of existence.

If you have got none, I will share a basic one

And it is simple:

Be one with your higher self

To be truthful to yourself

To shed your ego and

Be capable to find and respect

The godly element in every life (including yours).

Kaleidoscope of My Soul

Pieces of me merge into the dense fog at the mountain top

I decide to cut myself deep and bleed dry to write my poetry

As a kid, I loved the heroes but as an adult I understand the villains

I sense the joys of genuine laughters and the despair of the voids

I know where / how demons are created and reside in caverns

I feel my silently existing darkness walk away step by step and

I see blindingly bright colors through the kaleidoscope of my soul

I think I am now in love with being alive and being one with my higher self.

<u>*Welcomed Hope*</u>

Lines are drawn today for us to disappear within

Open your heart wide enough to hide and seek within

A sojourn passing through caverns of soul is called for

By the limitlessness that lies on the other side

How do you measure success after reaching there

Our legacy and distance travelled will be left behind

For now, I have conquered my fears and welcomed hope

Into this minuscule head space that is miles away

From all platforms that want to feed me

Antagonism draped in utmost care.

<u>*Theory Excogitated*</u>

I excogitate a theory for myself

A vivid perception of my own rises

I find an innerstanding amongst

All information tossed my way

If I surrender to this call of malaise

This putrid present I am surrounded by

Will drown me sluggishly to a black hole

I will smell like an unapologetic contrition

Consequencing into a catastrophe next morning.

Springing of the Spring

Caught into the web of cyclical events

I am held captive by the stems that

Await the blooms at their end

With Spring springing in this air

It is my time to become me from

My umbrage of others' perceptions

It is my time to get sober from

All the times I have been drunk on life

I will meet me again in peace

My welts finally learnt to blossom.

Epiphanies in Depths of Isolation

In a world already on its knees

Everyone is looking for their sky

To look high up and watch their moon

A subtle reminder of a constant in life

In times like these, I get her cuddles

She holds me higher than my higher self

In the depths of isolation lies realizations

> — Time has come to shift consciousness to the back of our heads and measure the depths of our quantum realm dreams

> — To use our lucid dreams to contact other forms of intelligence and

> — To discover our own Sirius and personal Stargate

Secret of/to Immortality

Your body is your DNA like a genie in a bottle except

They are genes in your body connected to unified field of the Universe

They react to your thoughts to make them reality

Your body is your brain accepting inputs that reprogram it

You can learn to control it and utilize it as unifying field

Between physical, emotional and mental bodies

It will be an accelerated path to psycho-spiritual mastery

Your body is a frequency and God's frequency exists in you

Use it to heal everything unresolved in your energy

Your body is a spirit connected (at all times) to the Source

A union of these produces a mastery called Life

Learn about the mastery and you will discern the secret of/to Immortality.

In a World of Selfies

In this world filled with selfies

People lack knowledge of self

This consequences to dis-ease

It will capture and emit lower vibrations

(like negativity, criticism and judgements)

Learn to vibrate at a higher state

Operate out of love and compassion

To be happy in who you truly are

Attract authenticity, not illusion

This will awaken the sleeping warrior within

For an open pineal gland is a truth detector

It will pick up subtle inconsistencies

Of lies and subliminal messages

Used to conceal every true intention

Change is inevitable but transformation

Happens with a conscious choice

Remember:

Beautiful are those whose brokenness

Births transformation and wisdom.

I Journey with Me

Society wants to fill me with misery

Till it bleeds through my eyes

I see its red raw eyes grip my neck

To hold it open and pour demon blood

Its pure evil saves me the translation

Its words whisk away with the wind

Before it can feel the touch of my ears

I am a fulcrum to a flawless sunshine

I journey with me to find me again and

Not be lost in heaviness of everydays.

Battle of God and Devil

The battle of God and Devil is inside of you

God and God particle are not floating around

For humanity to placate and beg for help

With cheap, frivolous and superficial offerings

God particle is a connection of the Source

Living quietly and deeply within you

Cultivate it so God's power can act through you

Use the God particle to conquer your lower demons

Be one with your divine self through forces of nature

That reside within than looking for it in books.

Duality: A State of Separation

Duality is truly a state of separation

It is the opposite of your current reality

Your ego seeks to divide and separate

Your soul seeks to unify and heal

Darkness and light are both of one nature

Different only in seeming

For each arises from the Source

Darkness is disorder and light is order

Darkness transmuted is the light of the Light

Knowledge of self lights the way away from darkness and

Becomes a compass to master your divine powers.

Ego vs. Soul

Ego seeks to serve itself; Soul seeks to serve others

Ego is drawn to lust; Soul is drawn to love

Ego seeks outward recognition; Soul seeks inner authenticity

Ego feels lack; Soul feels abundance

Ego seeks to preserve self; Soul seeks to preserve others

Ego sees life as a competition; Soul sees life as a gift

Ego is mortal; soul is eternal

Ego seeks knowledge; Soul seeks wisdom

Ego enjoys the prize; Soul enjoys the journey

Ego is a cause to pain; Soul is a cause to healing

Ego rejects God; Soul embraces God

Ego seeks to be filled; Soul is eternal wholeness

Ego is mine; Soul is we!

Greed to Gratitude

Life is not happening to you

It is merely reacting to you

Transform greed into gratitude

Do not fight the past

Build something new

Be the cause of an effect

Not the effect of a cause

Observe without evaluation

Do not observe opinions

If you know who you are

Knowing all other will not matter!

Reality While Being Awoke

I drove away from the wet pavement shore

And lost the signal to the chaotic world

As final goodbyes kindled the fire inside

I commenced my long-awaited journey

Towards the arrant certitude of singularity

I channeled my hysteria and ardor to purge fret

My mind sight created a limpid lens to observe

The truth to create my reality while being awoke.

Enlightenment: A Rather Destructive Process

Enlightenment is a destructive process

It is not concerned with being better

It is not about being happier than before

Enlightenment is crumbling away of untruth

It is the ability to see through the façade of pretense

It is the complete eradication of

Everything you imagined to be true

It is the realization that you no longer

Fir the norm and know what you are truly made of

It is when you become the radio receiver through which

The voice of the Universe is transmitted.

Substance of Soul

Black shades surround me

I feel existence of everything

With sheer blank and nothingness

Splendor of light is now

A memory of the day and

A solid gloom closes up

The menial deeds of the day

Will now be washed away

As the night shares its wisdom

Life as a I know is no longer

A continued weariness and despair

Right (now) here is a start to divinity

The true substance of the soul.

<u>Existence of Time</u>

Have you pondered if Time really exists?

Time does not exist, only clocks exist

Time is just an agreed upon construct

Distance is taken and divided in segments

(one rotation of Earth, one orbit of Sun)

These segments are then given labels

While this labeling may have its uses

Do not be programmed to live your life

By this construct (as if it were real)

Do not confuse this shared construct

With something that is tangible and

Thus, become its slave.

Spirituality and Religion

Spirituality does not come from religion

It comes from each breath of the soul

Stop confusing spirituality with religion

Religion is set of rules, regulations and

Rituals created by humans that were

Supposed to help people spiritually

Human imperfections has made religion

Corrupt, political, divisive and

Merely a tool for power struggle

Spirituality is not theology or ideology

It is simply a way of life (most original)

In the purest as given by the Source

Spirituality is a link of networks

Connecting us to the Source, Universe, and each other.

— *Words of Emperor Selassie I*

Courage: My Armor

Watered by memories, emotions grow from the soil of my heart

The not happy ones, I pluck and uproot to avoid their rebirth

They feed on the memories of the past that I am at to demolish

Break the chains link by link, crumble the wall brick by brick

Collapse hurdles bit by bit, my mind will no longer shut

Deeply rooted in the soil of my soul, love will grow ceaselessly

Emerging from pit of darkness resurrecting like a phoenix

My love will bloom heroically with hope as my power and

Courage as my armor to witness my fight and awakening.

<u>*Intuition: Your Inner Tuition*</u>

Intuition is your inner tuition

It teaches you from inside out

To find it, tune in within yourself

It is the frequency of your higher self

And not a reflection of your thoughts

Clear the fearful 'what ifs' of the mind

To allow intuition to freely speak

Seek all answers in that inner-net

For intuitive knowledge is authentic

And fundamentally tuned to your natural being.

Stair Steps to Ascension

The night's empty canvas eludes me to

The promise of knowledge I made to self

My soul grows spiritually while in human form

All lessons are stair steps to enable my ascension

Authenticity is not a consequence

Rather a requirement at the start line

As night transforms into light again

My environmentally conditioned robot skin is shed

And I am now a unique expression

That equates to my being of a

Primeval universal intelligence

That cannot be created or destroyed.

The Real Poison

Poison is what harms well being

It causes illness and death

It can be a substance or a toxin

Venom or bane or a contagion even

But I can also be anything beyond

That is needed by body and soul

It can be the wall of ego that prevents

You from getting close to the truth

It can be some deep-rooted fears

Instilled by loud lies of bogus institutions

It can be your laziness to search facts

That will consequence in ignorance

Be wise and change your mindset

Do not let poison infiltrate your universe

Make energy your first language

It will always choose the right frequency.

Shades of Presence

Presence is being present in a place or thing

It is often associated with being stationed but

There is more to it than meets the eye

Presence is incomplete without a union of

Grounding and tranquility in this very moment

It demands both, physical and spiritual awareness

With emotional acceptance and mental alertness

The participation of consciousness in the here and now

With the ability to sense and feel the frequency

Which is accepted yet awaits the decision of absorption

Be your own energy and vibrations of the soul.

Faces of Revolution

Revolution is activity or movement

Designed to effect fundamental changes

In any given socio-economic situation

It broadens the world to fit you

It challenges your comfort for sacrifice

It also questions your forms of compromise

It has many forms of expression

It is to educate ourselves appropriately

It is about posts made on social media

It is coming down to streets for protests

It is about sharing resources and donating silently

It is crucial conversations with friends and family

More importantly, revolution is also from within

To clean the enormous junk that

Constantly clutters your mind

Learn to collect your thoughts and

Cultivate the magical power in this

Infinite field of consciousness.

Universe to Uni-verse

Meditation is not about controlling your mind and thoughts

It is more about mindfulness and focusing your mind

It is to choose to make room for silence amidst the noise

It is information that talks to your soul and DNA

It is to let go your fear to see past your sight onto your vision

It is to perfect the art to manifest what you want

It is to find stillness in your movement of time and space

It is isolation in seclusion to get your soul right

It is to enter altered state of consciousness that transform you

It is a path to wisdom that all phenomena is one: uni-verse.

<u>*Every Day*</u>

In times when your friends turn the other way

I love mine every day

In times when past conditioning rules the present

I shed mine every day

In times when souls are stolen and disowned

I save mine every day

In times when upward going steps are destroyed

I create mine every day

In times when logic is filled with illusion

I develop mine every day

In times when loneliness screams back at you

I heal myself every day.

My Fight for Change

In my fight for change:

My tolerance past its expiration date

My will summoned to make a difference

Their malice intent spoken aloud

My heart broken by their sword of rage

My poetry written to bandage my wound

Letters and words; my hand grenade

Their incubus now royally defeated

This victory is mine to keep and cherish

Till my being is questioned and haunted again.

Check Your Season

Outer season is mostly same for many

Check if your inner season is alike

It is the cusp of summer on the outside

Check if your thoughts are flowering

The sky is painted in cerulean blue shades

Check if your heart is insouciant

The seasonings are sprinkled on fruits

Check if your soul is fruiting of ecstasy

Everything around is efflorescent

Check if your being's horizons are expanding beyond.

Who am I?

My birthplace is love

My existence is truth

My language is poetry

My speech is emotion

My sense is energy

My feeling is gratitude

My guide is intuition

My practice is meditation

My souls is immortal

My being is eternal.

East-West, Left-Right

Do not believe all that your stained eyes tell you

With some reality they show limitations too

In the east they notice some shuddering grime

In the west they observe their ego in shattered mirrors

On the left they witness thunder roars from their azure

On the right they hear their shaky whispering voices

Feel the vibrations and energy of your higher faculties

Open your third eye and recognize your potential

In the east you will notice hope budding from grime

In the west you will observe humility thrive through mirrors

On the left you will witness birds chirping in the azure

On the right you will hear truth in your intuition's voices.

<u>*Purge to Keep*</u>

You leave the garden
But keep the fragrance

You leave the photograph
But keep the beauty

You leave the sea
But keep the salt

You leave the trails
But keep the path

You leave the city
But keep the streets

You leave the friend
But keep the memories

You leave the home
But keep the heart

You leave the body
But keep your experiences

You leave the emotions
But keep the soul.

Dashboards, Scorecards and Catalogs

Today mankind carries dashboards

Containing visuals of variety of lies and grief

Strategies following to convert it to joyous bliss

Today mankind carries scorecards

Maintaining score of highs and lows

Analyzing trends of metrics designed to lead to utopia

Today mankind carries catalogs

Consisting of lists and pictures of places to travel

Trying to find happiness on other side of the globe

Today, let go of that heavy baggage

Acquit yourself from yesterday's agony

Pardon yourself from gruesome mistakes

Release all that eclipses your happiness

Discharge yourself from every day's drudgery and

Live life with a purpose of erasing evil that comes hereafter.

Wipes of Forgiveness

Sentenced by sunshine

Dreams were thawed

Intuition was watered

And it became my GPS

Rugged lands walked upon

Socks found tattered

Now, I look spent and old

Every day adds a wrinkle

On my fresh yet old soul

My journey only continues

As forgiveness (once again) wipes out

All my hurt and agony away.

Putting Past to Rest

I bury the body of a fallen decade

Put it to rest where it was meant to be

Ghosts of my past that walked with me

No longer in presence and now far away

It is said that hindsight is twenty-twenty

I can for once clearly see the past of

Where I have been, how I have been

Places I have travelled, how I have grown and

Most importantly who I have become

She has patiently waited for me

She has walked my path with me

Hand in hand she helped me purge

All that was an encumbrance

She has freed me to joyfully sing

The song of happiness and freedom

That I sang on days beyond recall.

Darkness: My True Well Wisher

Darkness is my true well wisher

It powers my inner light and love

I whisper in the ears of passing winds

Silence answers back through my epiphanies

I walked out of all relation (but one with her)

Saying I have done all I can do here

This left behind a famine saving my tears

To water the seeds of personal growth.

Shores of Destiny

On the shores of destiny

I stand on sand made of fate

I write down my quiddity

Using a broken stick that knows

With every wave of experience

Within moments, this too will

Reduce to a treasured past

My torpid stick pleads for mercy

But how can I bestow that compassion

When I vowed optimism and hope

Till my last heartbeat loses its breath.

Ownership of Self

Everything from our lives to professions are governed by

National institutes which are designed human inventions

To monopolize power and enslave mankind

I mull upon the existence of such institutes

The innerstanding comes from studying history

Slave patrols and night watchers shaping into police

To control behavior of the minority transformed to slaves

All in the name of maintaining economic order and

Assisting wealthy landowners to own slaves as property

Self-imposed state of slavery plays a part too

The key to break this ever-rising trend of slavery is

Knowledge of self that makes people unfit to be slaves

Growth and change are painful, but nothing is as painful as

Remaining enslaved by lies, slander, abuse, hatred and

Agreed upon construct (concepts) of select few in power

Tap into the power of beyond all boundaries

Work towards creating a quantum shift in human consciousness

To become free and find lasting ownership of self.

Solitude: My Guiding Light

Solitude guides me on my path to self

Within my wild heart I open my eyes

To search the truth in dark waters

I am greeted by curiosity dipped in ardor

With a whiff of uncommon courage:

I download wisdom that the North holds

I send love to (my) South that needs healing

Energy clears and moves through the East

Emotions purify and transforms the West.

A Profound Conversation

Do not destroy my (well believed) illusions, commanded Fear

I will spread my positivity and positive vibes all around, Energy said with conviction

I will cast my spells all over those vibes, snapped Words

I will light the lamp inside this temple, softly replied Life.

<u>Cause and Effect</u>

Consumerism causes superficiality

Superficiality causes cravings

Cravings cause clinging

Clinging causes attachments

Attachment causes identification

Identification causes entanglement

Entanglement causes confusion

Confusion causes frustration

Frustration causes anger

Anger causes suffering

Suffering from such suffering

(Ask yourself) is it worth it?

Activate Airplane Mode

I activate my airplane mode

To admire the lake side

Beaches are way too salty and

Lake views assiduously teach

The importance of reflection

It is intrinsic to a world

Where imbroglio is nonexistent

And love is spread copiously.

<u>Under Moonlight Blanket</u>

I sit on the roof of the sky wrapped in my moonlight blanket

I lend darkest colors of my contorted complexities to the night

Stars offer rather simplistic birds' eyes view perspectives in exchange

Suddenly I catch myself amidst insomnia and awakened mind

I watch angels birthing from the laughing demons on my inside

My creativity steps out of buried coffin to begin its march in my direction

On the way, it shrugs off the decay and braces itself to experience

Its journey of forming words on paper from concepts of the mind that

Suffering is the golden cross upon which the rose of soul unfolds.

Hashtags

In times where hashtags are more popular than your own feelings

The expectation is to place as many hashtags hoping people read words

This makes me wonder if any feelings are (actually) being shared and felt

Can hashtags ever create compassion required to innerstand emotions?

Can hashtags elucidate the ongoing war between the heart, mind and soul?

Can hashtags replace my hour-long conversation with my twin flame?

Can hashtags illustrate her circumstances and her place in them?

To me hashtags are merely a way to direct this generation to my poetry

That decodes the soul's journey in the story of life and inspire a dialog

To communicate, express and empathize with what humankind encounters.

Lost in Light

Blame the accidents on the fiery sunrise

Gawk into the burning pupils of the sun

No silver lining can ever be found there

My skin and flesh will start burning as

The flooding light slowly buries the dark

My expertise is manifesting contours

From the vastness of the night dark and

Not be the architecture silhouettes in light

I am found in the dark afloat on the water

I am lost in the light and my perspective disappears

I unapologetically do not fear darkness

For my light shines from within.

My Autumn

Adulthood in the landscapes will flare soon

Colors all around will set everything ablaze

Cooler temperatures will caress my being

As the sun will sprawl slightly beyond my reach

I feel maturity will slowly inch towards me

I will sound wise in my writings and doings

This time Autumn will carry me a little higher

Than I could have ever aspired for on my own.

Thank Your Previous Versions

Step away from demands of daily life

Disconnect from the internal monologs that

Beckon you away from this presence

Do not be scattered into the panic and survival mode

Free yourself from the cages in your own mind

Submit to the sweet promises that mindfulness makes

Be grateful for all the previous versions of you

Remember, being vulnerable helps the healing

Heal all the brokenness and hurt from over the years

How we feel creates our world and experiences

You are a human magnet that attracts

Everything you speak, think, and feel.

True Cleansing

Trees shed their foliage to the sounds of logic in the
background

Similarly,

I valiantly exuviate my forced need to be perfect all the time

With that I peel off layers of self-doubt prisoned in my rib cage

I courageously ask insecurity to stop guarding my house

I let go of other people's expectations I had locked in a jar

I doff my jacket dipped in colors of all things I cannot control

My newly gained confidence is laced with self-care and love

In this season of adulthood and reasoning, I set myself free of

Anything that does not belong to the engravings on my veins.

Today Came with No Labels

Trust the timings of the happenings of your life

Leave the world of yesterdays and tomorrows

Live the here and the present of this present day

It has no labels and no definitions because

It is simple (and pure) at heart and true to its form

Add a little more ordinary

An extra ordinary human being is what you will become

Fight the friendly faces that hold monsters inside

Welcome the angels full of scars with open arms

Embrace the transitions as you walk the Experience Avenue

And find yourself growing up to the sounds of

Empathy, kindness, humanity, love and logic.

Darkness: Ground of Creation

Rustling leaves demand to listen my heart's murmur

Blue skies command to see my efforts to a renewed chance

Brisk winds dictate me to share my gestated truths

Unadopted roads urge me to vocalize my battles fought

They all comprehend my reality is rooted in darkness

For them darkness is a low state of mind founded in evil

But little do they know darkness is where goodness births

Darkness is where a seed in the ground transforms to sprout

Darkness is where a new life is carried by a mother

Darkness is where eyes are shut, and meditation happens

Darkness is where night skies witness promises of better tomorrows

Darkness is, indeed, a throbbing and breeding ground of creation.

Before Life Engulfs Again

The most beautiful hues of orange and red shine on us

Slowly it will be time for us to enter the duskiness around us

Let us slowly learn to not choke on other people's smoke

Let us silence the never-ending sound of worthlessness

Let us make the laughing demons crawl out of our skins

Let us drive without direction to a destination unknown

Let us feel safe in the vastness of that wilderness

Keep other thoughts at bay long enough to regain strength

Before life devours us and engulfs us again.

Rising of Crimson Banner

Dreams, like my past are

Faded but not forgotten

There is no ground in it

Only currents of my being

Never-ending steps of

An unforgotten strength

Rights my broken spirit

In land beyond memories

As crimson banner rises

The horizon is ablaze

Now, slowly wake and follow

Along this trail of effulgence.

Actions Stand Sovereign

Under the mascara skies

In the company of trees

I see my ancestors live

Through the life in my bones

I hear my progenitors

Through the wind's whispers

I feel my forefathers

Through the wisdom waters

Their feats of actions

Inevitably define my fate

But I am ready to let go

And let my actions

(Solely) stand sovereign.

<u>*Why Behind Wounds*</u>

Have you simply wondered

How temporary people live

The permanent of all lessons

I have been wounded before

Wound is the place where

Light enters to reach the inside

It happens so you lose someone

To find a part of your (lost) self

Your mind should be stronger

Than the emotions you feel

In a world of masked faces

You are (then) able to see a soul.

Winning Made Easy

Crawling in open spaces

Challenging my credentials

Learning susceptibility

Creating fancied opportunities

Making harsh commitments

Empowering shifts in the gear

Going through the process

Trusting my own experiences

Breaking chains of the past

Pleasing none but myself

Seeing myself with new outlook

Winning each time is now easy.

Leave Behind, March Towards

I leave behind the miles of suffering nostalgia

I embrace the aspirations that lie deep within

I leave behind the gray winter of my heart

I march towards the warm spring of my soul

This new time is more of a map than a destination.

Later: A Luxury Word

Later is a luxury word

People in hurry cannot afford

I am in a state of calmness

See the storm of tranquility

Feel the stillness of transition

Witness the spells of silence

Start over on the inside

Transform my happenstance

Transmogrify my repute.

<u>*Traipse in the Mountains*</u>

A traipse in the mountains is where loneliness exists

In the climb is where spirits whisper their guarded secrets

A discourse with them is how I anatomize my real footings

Enhanced perspectives and a state of trance is what I gain

Deep from the web of being is where I will ascent from

The space between life, death and fate is where I will live and

Neat box of defined character is how I will be penned in the history books.

One Day at a Time

One act of kindness and I will grow a million ways on the inside

One minute at the beach and I will collect a million crunchy particles of sand

One sunset by the mountains and I will spend a million minutes watching

One glance at stars above and I will illuminate a million times

One last breath before time will stop and ask me a million questions

One answer and I will be redeemed, "I know I tried my best one day at a time."

Not Lost

When life puts you under pressure

Trace its ridges in your pocket

Smell its piney scent on your shirt

Hum its anthem under your breath

But after you have done all of that

Sit down at the set of the sun

Count your blessings you have

Count all the things you have done

If that is zilch through lifelong day

And no sunshine smile is brought on

Remind yourself: No act is small

Get up, go out and help a soul

It may cost nothing at all and

If you are unable to that small act

Count your day as worse, not lost.

About the Author

Being a twin meant to not only have a mirror to grow up with but also to have an action-packed childhood. Jhanjhri grew up in India and now is a California native. Her passion for poetry can be traced back to her pre-professional days. Whether as an elementary school student participating in poetry writings or elocution competitions in college years, she has always expressed herself in form of poems. She wrote poems on various subjects for a leading Indian newspaper 'The Times of India'. Jhanjhri now writes about human feelings swimming around inside the heart, the uphill battle to perseverance and healing, and immense happiness felt by being one with one's higher self.

Lightning Source UK Ltd.
Milton Keynes UK
UKHW011141190721
387406UK00002B/639